W0360663

Speakeasy Activities 6e

A1+ ▶ A2

Coordination pédagogique de l'ouvrage :
Ruth Alimi
IA-IPR, Académie de Créteil

Avec la contribution de :
Marie-Christine Delsinne
Collège Denecourt, Bois-le-Roi (77)
Formatrice, Académie de Créteil

Stéphanie Brousse-Crescent

Cécile Clavilier
Collège La Nacelle, Corbeil-Essonnes (91)
Formatrice, Académie de Versailles

Violaine Dandine
Collège Albert Camus, Perpignan (66)

Isabelle Garnier
Collège de la Clé Saint-Pierre, Elancourt (78)

Yvelise Montagliani
Collège Flora Tristan, Paris (75)

Krystell Rouméas
Collège et Lycée Saint-Michel de Picpus, Saint-Mandé (94)

Pascal Vinson
Collège Pilâtre de Rozier, Paris (75)
Formateur, Académie de Paris

Jennifer Wattrelot
Collège Renée Taillefer, Gaillac (81)

Nathan

La 6e est la 3e année du cycle 3 instauré par les nouveaux programmes de la réforme des collèges applicables à partir de la rentrée 2016. Ce cycle regroupe les classes de CM1, CM2 et 6e.

En fin de cycle 3, tous les élèves doivent avoir atteint le niveau A1 dans les 5 activités langagières et le niveau A2 dans au moins deux activités langagières.

Activité langagière	ÉCOUTER ET COMPRENDRE	LIRE	RÉAGIR ET DIALOGUER	PARLER EN CONTINU	ÉCRIRE ET RÉAGIR À L'ÉCRIT
A1	Peut comprendre des mots familiers et des expressions courantes sur lui-même, sa famille et son environnement.	Peut comprendre, des textes courts et très simples, phrase par phrase, en relevant des noms, des mots familiers et des expressions très élémentaires et en relisant si nécessaire.	Peut interagir brièvement dans des situations déjà connues en utilisant des mots et expressions simples et avec un débit lent.	Peut produire des expressions simples, isolées, sur les gens et les choses.	Peut écrire des expressions et phrases simples isolées.
A2	Peut comprendre une intervention brève si elle est claire et simple.	Peut comprendre de courts textes simples sur des sujets concrets courants avec une fréquence élevée de langue quotidienne.	Peut interagir avec une aisance raisonnable dans des situations bien structurées et de courtes conversations à condition que le locuteur apporte de l'aide le cas échéant.	Peut décrire ou présenter simplement des gens, des conditions de vie, des activités quotidiennes, ce qu'on aime ou pas, par de courtes séries d'expressions ou de phrases.	Peut écrire une série d'expressions et de phrases simples reliées par des connecteurs simples tels que « et », « mais » et « parce que ».

Les trois parcours des nouveaux programmes

Dans les nouveaux programmes, les apprentissages s'inscrivent dans **3 parcours** qui donnent du sens aux apprentissages :

Le parcours citoyen Parcours citoyen fait des élèves des personnes responsables.

Le parcours artistique Parcours artistique sensibilise les élèves à toutes les formes d'art.

Le parcours avenir Parcours avenir permet de préparer son orientation professionnelle.

Édition : Seonaid Cruickshank, assistée de Margot Pastier
Iconographie : Nathalie Bencal
Illustrateurs : Nicolas Paillard de Chesnay, Claude-Henri Saunier
Conception de la maquette : Frédéric Jely
Mise en page : Domino
Conception de la couverture : Frédéric Jély

© Éditions Nathan 2016
ISBN 978.2.09.174156.7

DANGER LE PHOTOCOPILLAGE TUE LE LIVRE

*« Le photocopillage, c'est l'usage abusif et collectif de la photocopie sans autorisation des auteurs et des éditeurs.
Largement répandu dans les établissements d'enseignement, le photocopillage menace l'avenir du livre, car il met en danger son équilibre économique. Il prive les auteurs d'une juste rémunération.
En dehors de l'usage privé du copiste, toute reproduction totale ou partielle de cet ouvrage est interdite. »*

Sommaire

The Simpsons, America's First Family

Activity 1 Meet the Simpsons

A **Look at this poster. How much do you know about *The Simpsons*? Brainstorm vocabulary and complete the following mind map:**

Describing Someone

- Other
- Hair
- Eyes
- Character
- Clothes

B **Select a character from the poster and describe him/her:**

He/she is ... • He/she has got ... • On the poster he/she is ... •
Usually, he/she ... • I like him/her because I find him/her ...

Learn as You Wish

Pour te préparer à décrire un personnage oralement, choisis la méthode que tu préfères, A ou B.
Écris au crayon afin de que tu puisses te corriger si nécessaire.

A 1. Comparer avec le français. Comment dis-tu les expressions suivantes quand tu parles avec tes amis ?

Je ne sais pas : .... Je ne veux pas : ....

Je veux : .... Je n'ai pas :...

MP3 **2. Écoute et lis les phrases suivantes. Barre les lettres qui ne se prononcent pas.**

Example: *she is = she's – he has got = he's got*

He is a big boy.
She has got beautiful hair.
He likes eating and reading.
She has not got blue hair.
He is not tall.
He does not like ice cream.

3. Reprends la description de ton personnage (Activité 1B) sans écrire les lettres qui ne se prononcent pas.

MP3 **B 1. Certains mots de ta description doivent être plus accentués que d'autres. Écoute les phrases et entoure les mots accentués.**

2. Relis ta description du personnage (Activité 1B) en entourant les mots accentués.

TIPS

MP3 *N'oublie pas que ta voix doit descendre en fin de phrases. Répète ta description jusqu'à ce que tu sois satisfait(e).*

Activity 2 Who's Who?

Play "Who's Who?" with your partner.
Pick a character from the list below and get ready to answer your partner's questions with short answers. Then swap roles and ask your partner yes/no questions to discover his/her character.

The Simpson family: Homer, Marge, Lisa, Maggie and Bart, with their dog, Santa's Little Helper

Krusty the Clown

Groundskeeper Willie

Principal Skinner

Mr Burns with Homer Simpson

Is he/she ... ? Yes, he/she is. / No he/she isn't.
Has he/she got ... ? Yes, he/she has. / No, he/she hasn't.
Does he/she ... ? Yes, he/she does. / No, he/she doesn't.

Activity 3 Describing the Characters

How well do you know The Simpsons?

A For each sentence, circle the correct answer:

1. Maggie never talks: she is chatty / quiet / unfriendly.
2. Lisa plays the saxophone like a pro: she's talented / ambitious / silly.
3. Bart loves skateboarding: he's studious / sporty / polite.
4. Homer never remembers important things: he is clever / adorable / forgetful.
5. Mr Burns is really mean to everyone: he's evil / generous / sensitive.

B Pair Work

Pupil A Do Activity 3.B. on this page. Pupil B Your Activity 3.B. is on page 62.

Pupil A

Read the description and guess who the character is:

He is in his forties, he is married and has three children. He works in a nuclear power plant. He is overweight and almost bald. He is forgetful and very lazy. His favourite things to eat are raspberry cream doughnuts! He also loves spending time with his friends and watching TV. His name is:..

C Prepare questions to help you find out who your partner's character is. Ask about the character's:

a. Looks?
b. Age?
c. Family?
d. Personality?
e. Likes and dislikes?
f. Hobbies?

Activity 4 The Simpsons are the Best!

Complete this paragraph using the superlatives from the box.

biggest • craziest • meanest • most popular • smartest • worst

Bart is the .... of all the Simpsons characters and Krusty is probably the .... character of all. He's horrible! Moe has the .... bar in Springfield. It's enormous! Homer probably works for the .... boss in the world. Lisa is the .... character in the series and Marge has the .... hair of all!

Activity 5 Expressing Opinions

MP3 **A** **1. Match up these words with their pronunciation.**

a. awesome
b. evil
c. favourite
d. hilarious
e. addictive
f. annoying

I. /ə'dɪktɪv/
II. /'feɪvərɪt/
III. /hɪ'lɛərɪəs/
IV. /'ɔːsəm/
V. /'iːvl/
VI. /ə'nɔɪɪŋ/

MP3 **2. Sort the words according to the prononciation of <o>.**

show • popular • loud • most • mouth • though • would • love • cool • son • who • become • Homer

əʊ	aʊ	ɒ	uː	ʊ	ʌ

MP3 **B** **Listen to the audio and fill in the table below.**

Character's name	Number of votes	Reasons

C **Complete the following text.**

The most popular Simpsons character is .... because he/she is .... and .... I agree / disagree because I think ....

Activity 6

Read Milhouse's ID card and complete the paragraph with the missing words.

SPRINGFIELD, OR.
ID CARD

First name: Milhouse
Surname: Van Houten
Age: 10
Family: only child
Height: short
Hair: straight, blue
Personality: loyal, clumsy
Job/Occupation: 4th grade pupil - Springfield Elementary School
Hobbies: spending time with Bart and Lisa, riding his bicycle
Particularity: thick glasses

This is ...., he is .... years old.

Milhouse doesn't have any brothers or sisters, he is an .... child.

Milhouse is ...., his hair is .... and .... and he wears .... He is Bart's most .... friend, but he is the .... pupil in school!

His hobbies are .... and .... his ....

Your Task Create a Character

Create your own Simpsons character!
Complete your character's ID card.
Finally, be ready to present your character to the class!

SPRINGFIELD, OR.
ID CARD

First name: ....
Surname: ....
Age: ....
Family: ....
Height: ....
Hair: ....
Personality: ....
Job/Occupation: ....
Hobbies: ....

The Leprechaun and the Pot of Gold

Activity 1 Describing Magical Creatures

A **1. Put the adjectives in the correct columns.**

small • big • tall • short • long

XS/S	L/XL

2. Link the words to the corresponding details in the pictures.

a pointed hat • pointed shoes • a long dress • a beard • long hair • short hair

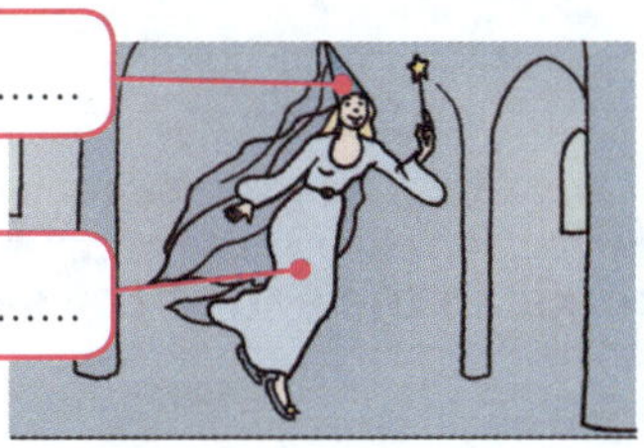

3. Listen and write the name of the character under the correct picture:

a banshee • a giant • a leprechaun • a fairy • an elf

B **Play "Who is it?" Prepare five yes/no questions to ask your partner to guess which character he/she selected from A.3. Then get ready to answer his/her questions with short answers.**

Example:

A: " Is it a boy?" **B:** "No, it isn't."

A: "Has she got long hair?" **B:** "Yes, she has."

Activity 2 Listening to a Legend

A Listen to Part 1. Tick the correct answer.

1. This legend is about: ☐ elves ☐ leprechauns ☐ fairies ☐ banshees ☐ giants.
2. This legend comes from: ☐ Wales ☐ Scotland ☐ Ireland ☐ England.
3. The creatures live in: ☐ magical fountains ☐ magical mountains.

B Listen to Part 2 and tick the sentences that are correct.

☐ **1. a.** A girl was looking for a leprechaun.
☐ **b.** A leprechaun was looking for a girl.
☐ **c.** A girl was looking for her sheep.

☐ **2. a.** The girl found her sheep.
☐ **b.** The girl found a leprechaun.

☐ **3. a.** The leprechaun is a big man.
☐ **b.** The leprechaun is a little man.

☐ **4. a.** The girl took the leprechaun's sheep.
☐ **b.** The leprechaun took the girl's hat.
☐ **c.** The girl took the leprechaun's hat.

☐ **5. a.** The girl wants the leprechaun's pot of hats.
☐ **b.** The girl wants the leprechaun's pot of gold.

☐ **6. a.** The girl must keep the leprechaun's hat.
☐ **b.** The girl must keep the leprechaun's secret.

C 1. Choose the picture that corresponds to the end of the story.

☐ 

☐ 

2. Complete the sentence.

The girl was .... all of her life.

Learn as You Wish

Pour écrire une légende, choisis A ou B.

A Choisir le lexique. Regarde les dessins de la rubrique Your Task, puis surligne, dans le nuage de mots ci-dessous, les mots dont tu auras besoin pour écrire l'histoire. N'oublie pas d'utiliser également les expressions que tu as vues dans l'Activité 1.

big sad giant dessert tall
long husband fat great trousers get married become
chef very small hungry mashed potatoes ever after
hot fall in love kitchen table wife chicken soup
delicious dress happy shoes prepare

B Respecter les différentes étapes du récit. Écris une légende en choisissant les éléments que tu préfères dans chacune des étapes de l'histoire.

Situation initiale Indique où et quand se passe l'histoire, qui est le personnage principal, ce qu'il fait et qui il rencontre.

☐ Once upon a time, ☐ One fine night, ☐ One day,
a ☐ man ☐ woman ☐ boy ☐ girl
was ☐ looking for his/her goats ☐ walking his/her dog
when he/she met a ☐ banshee ☐ fairy.

Déroulement de l'action Raconte le problème que rencontre l'un des personnages, ce que les personnages font et ce qu'ils se disent.

The ☐ man ☐ woman ☐ boy ☐ girl
took ☐ the banshee's hat ☐ the fairy's pointed shoe
and said: "If you want it back, ☐ tell me ☐ show me
where you ☐ keep ☐ put ☐ hide
your magic ☐ belt ☐ box."

Dénouement Imagine quelle solution résout le problème.

"Oh, no! ☐ I can't! ☐ It's impossible!,"
said the ☐ banshee ☐ fairy.
"But if you don't, I'll keep your ☐ hat ☐ pointed shoe
and you'll ☐ look ridiculous ☐ be cold".

Situation finale Explique quelle conséquence cette histoire a sur le personnage principal.

☐ Finally ☐ In the end,
the ☐ banshee ☐ fairy decided to share his/her secret
and the ☐ man ☐ woman ☐ boy ☐ girl
was happy ever after.

Your Task Writing a Story

Use Activities 1 and 2 to invent a story from the pictures. Each time you use an element from Activities 1 and 2, circle it.

Celebrating Guy Fawkes Night

Activity 1 Guy Fawkes Night in Pictures

The guy is burning on the bonfire.

Fireworks represent the explosion that Guy Fawkes wanted to create.

These people are taking the "guy", a representation of Guy Fawkes, to the bonfire.

Write questions about what you want to know about Guy Fawkes and Bonfire Night.

Guy Fawkes
- **who?**
- **famous, why?**

Bonfire Night
- **celebrated when?**
- **commemoration of?**
- **celebrated how?**

Here's the first question to get you started:
Who was Guy Fawkes? **If you need help with the questions,** **see page 14.**

....

....

....

Activity 2 Guy Fawkes History

Look at the pictures. They tell a story. Then read the sentences – they are not in the correct order. The transparent words will help you. Match the sentences with the corresponding pictures.

a. That's why today, on November 5th, people burn a Guy (Fawkes) on a bonfire and organise fireworks parties to celebrate the event.

b. In 1603, James I becomes King of Britain.

c. Robert Catesby (the leader of the plot) asks Guy Fawkes, an explosives expert, for some help.

d. The Parliament persuades James to introduce new laws against Catholics.

e. They hide 36 barrels of gunpowder under the Houses of Parliament.

f. So, in 1604, a group of Catholics decides to blow up the Houses of Parliament with explosives.

g. But the King discovers the plot and the conspirators are arrested on November 5th 1605.

Activity 3 Identifying a Suspect

Pupil A Do Activity 3 on this page.
Pupil B Your Activity 3 is on page 61.

Pupil A

A **You are going to role play a soldier interviewing a person who saw a strange man near Parliament. Prepare by writing the words in the correct boxes on the illustrations. Tick the correct adjectives.**

shoes • a jacket • a torch • a barrel • a beard • a moustache • a cape • boots • a sword • hat

TIPS
MP3 *Écoute les mots et entraîne-toi à les prononcer.*

B **Prepare four YES/NO questions to ask the witness about the person he/she saw.**

....

....

....

....

If you need help with the questions, you can do the Learn as You Wish activity on page 15.

C **Now ask your partner your questions and try to identify the picture he/she is describing.**

Learn as You Wish

Pour poser des questions, choisis la méthode que tu préfères, A ou B.

A Pose le plus de questions possible sur les images de l'activité 3. N'écris pas les questions mais répète-les plusieurs fois pour les mémoriser.

B Utilise les amorces ci-dessous pour préparer le plus de questions possible sur les images de l'activité 3.

YES/NO QUESTIONS

- clothes
  - Was the man/he wearing ....?
  - Did the man/he have .... on?
- objects
  - Was he holding .... in his arms / in his hand?
- body
- intonation ↗

TIPS

MP3 *Écoute les questions pour repérer leur intonation.*

Activity 4 Making a Guy

A **Watch the video.** @ CONNECT TO: collegien.nathan.fr/speak6

B **What do you need to make a "Guy"? Tick the right answers.**

- ☐ a coat
- ☐ newspaper
- ☐ a pullover
- ☐ a shirt
- ☐ trousers
- ☐ gloves
- ☐ a tie
- ☐ a scarf
- ☐ a jacket
- ☐ a cap
- ☐ a hat
- ☐ some string
- ☐ glue
- ☐ a marker pen
- ☐ a ball
- ☐ a shoe
- ☐ boots
- ☐ a balloon

C **Match the verbs with their translations.**

1. scrunch
2. tie
3. draw
4. put on
5. put in
6. make

- ☐ a. *fourrer / remplir*
- ☐ b. *dessiner*
- ☐ c. *froisser*
- ☐ d. *faire*
- ☐ e. *attacher*
- ☐ f. *mettre / passer (un vêtement)*

Your Task Present Guy Fawkes Night

Get ready to present Guy Fawkes Night. In your presentation:

1. Describe what happens on November 5th in England.
2. Explain what they celebrate.
3. Give some instructions on how to make a "Guy".

Breakfast

Activity 1 A Tongue Twister

MP3 **Listen to this breakfast tonguetwister. Can you say it?**

Yellow butter, purple jelly, red jam, black bread.
Spread it thick, say it quick!

Activity 2 Get Ready for an English Breakfast

MP3 **Do you remember these words? Listen. Can you find the missing letters?**

a • a • a • e • ea • ea • au • oo • aw • i • um • ma

to ....toes

b.......con

mushr.......ms

cr.......pets

b.......ked b.......ns

s....... sages

a bowl of cer....... l

a gl.......ss of m.......lk

str....... b.......rries

Learn as You Wish

MP3 **Pour apprendre le vocabulaire, choisis le texte rythmé que tu préfères, A ou B. Écoute-le puis entraine-toi à le dire.**

A A loaf of bread
• ● • ●
A jar of jam
• ● • ●
A jar of honey
• ● • ● •

B A loaf of bread
• ● • ●
A jar of jam
• ● • ●
Some tea and some milk
• ● • • ●
Some butter and some eggs
• ● • • • ●
Some bacon and some sausages.
• ● • • • ● • •
A bottle of orange juice
• ● • • ● • ●

Activity 3 What Do You Have in Your Kitchen?

MP3

A Underline the stressed syllables.

sugar

cocoa

pancakes

maple syrup

bananas

carrots

potatoes

broccoli

apples

oranges

grapefruit

croissants

peanut butter

B Write and draw the food you have in your cupboard and in your fridge.

cupboard

fridge

C You want to cook breakfast. Tell your partner what you have in your kitchen and what you would like for breakfast.

In my kitchen there is ...

For breakfast, I'd like...

D **Now ask your partner what he/she wants for breakfast.**

You	Your Partner
What would you like for breakfast? • Would you like...? • How about...?	Can I have ...? • I'd like... Yes, please • I'd prefer... • Sorry, I don't like...

E **Now write what your partner would like.**

For breakfast, my partner would like ....

....

....

Activity 4 Shopping List

What do you need to make breakfast for you and your partner? Write your shopping list.

Learn as You Wish

Pour apprendre le vocabulaire de la leçon, choisis la méthode que tu préfères A ou B :

A Classe les aliments par type.

Boissons	Aliments sucrés	Aliments salés

B Classe les aliments selon tes goûts.

☺	☹	?

TIPS

Tu peux ajouter des couleurs, coller des images, faire des dessins. Si cela te plaît, tu t'en souviendras mieux.

Activity 5 Containers

Can you match the name of the container with the correct picture?

TIPS
Lis à nouveau le texte rythmé page 16.

a can	a carton	a bottle	a packet	a jar

Activity 6 At the Supermarket

A What do they want to buy? Describe each trolley.

B What do you want to buy?
Say what's in your trolley. Then ask a friend about his/her trolley.

In my trolley there's / I have / I've got ...	In my friend's trolley there's ...

Activity 7 Jonathan Jones's Favourite Meal

A Read Jonathan's text.

My favourite meal by Jonathan

My favourite meal is breakfast. From Monday to Friday, I go to school early, so I have a quick breakfast. I usually have cereal with milk or sometimes I have toast and honey, but the weekend is different!
On Saturdays and Sundays, my dad cooks an English breakfast for everyone in our family. A typical English breakfast is eggs, bacon, sausages, tomatoes, mushrooms and baked beans (beans in tomato sauce). Then we have toast and honey. I drink orange juice and my mum and dad drink tea or coffee. I love breakfast at the weekend because I have it with my whole family.

B Jonathan's breakfast menu.

Circle the food he has on weekdays in red and the food he has at the weekend in blue.

C What do you have for breakfast? Write your breakfast menus.

On week days I have	At the weekend I have

Activity 8 What Does She Like Eating?

MP3

A Listen to Maggie.

1. What's her nationality?

☐ French ☐ American ☐ English ☐ Scottish ☐ Irish

2. Where is she living at the moment?

☐ France ☐ the U.S.A. ☐ England ☐ Scotland ☐ Ireland

3. She misses her country and its food. Which food does she miss the most?

☐ jelly ☐ cheesecake ☐ peanut butter ☐ pancakes

4. She loves... Write the names.

....

....

....

Activity 9 Use Your Imagination

You've moved to Mars and you are not very enthusiastic about Martian food. What do you miss the most?

I really miss

It's

Activity 10 What is Good for You?

A How many fruits and vegetables can you name?

tomatoes, ...

....

B A Poem

Listen and practise saying the poem.

I'm talkin' fruits and vegetables, 5 a Day!
1 -2 -3 -4 - 5 a Day
That's the fruit and vegetable way
Eat 5 servings every day
Say 5 a Day!
One! I grab a banana for my breakfast
Two! I eat a bunch of carrots for my lunch (Hey!)
Three! Feel a little hungry after school
An apple from the fridge and I'm on my way
Four! I have broccoli for dinner
Full of fibre with vitamins C and A
Five! I need just one more
Strawberries for dessert that's 5 a Day!

C What sort of food do you like the most? Write your favourite menu on the sandwich or in the apple.

Activity 11 Food Tennis

Play food tennis: Your partner says a food word or expression, then you say a food word or expression, etc. The winner is the player who doesn't stop.

Your Task Breakfast Role Play

Role-play in groups of 2 or 3.

Place: A Bed and Breakfast in an English-speaking country

Time: 8:00 am / breakfast time

Characters: 1 waiter/waitress + 2 tourists

Have fun!

TIPS

Rappelez-vous tous les échanges sur le petit-déjeuner.
Ne vous contentez pas de questions / réponses.

Breakfast Menu

A choice of cereal

Toast with butter, jam, honey or peanut butter

Pancakes with maple syrup

English Breakfast options:

Bacon
Sausage
Baked beans
Eggs
Mushrooms
Tomatoes

Hot drinks:

Tea
Coffee
Hot chocolate

Cold drinks:

Orange juice
Apple juice
Milk

Learn as You Wish

Pour apprendre le vocabulaire de la leçon, choisis la méthode que tu préfères A ou B :

A Recopie les mots nouveaux et fais un dessin pour t'en souvenir.

Exemple : 

a carton of milk

B Fais plusieurs listes de courses pour réemployer les mots nouveaux.

TIPS

MP3 *N'oublie pas d'écouter les mots et expressions enregistrés pour toi.*
Répète-les plusieurs fois.

White Christmas

Activity 1 Discovering a Story

A **Read this text. It is the first part of a story.**

December 24th

It's dark outside and it's getting colder and colder. Mike looks out of the window, there's nobody outside. It's Christmas Eve. Dad is in the kitchen preparing his special chocolate cookie recipe. Mike and Dad will have the cookies for dessert with some pecan ice cream, Mike's favourite, and they will watch a film on TV.

Tomorrow, Mike's aunt and uncle are coming with his two cousins, and Dad will cook ham with pineapple and there will be cheesecake for dessert. Then they will open their presents! This year Mike wants a skateboard… and the red package on top of the wardrobe looks big enough! And Mike has painted a portrait of his dad. Dad will like it.

B **Fill in Mike's diary with words from the text.**

December 24th – Christmas Eve!
Tonight, we're having real Christmas weather!
I can't wait for the meal!
………………… baked my favourite …………………: chocolate ………………… Yummy! And after dinner, I can ………………… my favourite film on TV.
Tomorrow is also going to be a lot of fun: my …………………………, ………………… and my ………………… are coming over. Lunch will be delicious! We'll have ………………… with ………………… and ………………… for dessert.
And everything will be home-made by my………………… He's …………………!
Then, the best moment: we'll exchange ………………… I'm really proud of the ………………… I made for ………………… this year: ………………… I'm not supposed to but I know what mine is. It's a ………………… Exactly what I wanted!

C Read the second part of the text.

Mike's dad doesn't talk much but he's a great dad: he listens carefully when Mike tells him about his problems at school, and they have fun in the summer when they go fishing together.
But Mike would like a mom. And Mike would like to have a brother or a sister or both.
Mom's photo is in a frame by Dad's bedside: in the photo, she is proudly holding a baby in her arms. Mike doesn't remember her, but Dad does. Once Mike asked him, "Dad, why don't you get married again?" Mike would like to have a mother like the woman who walks past their house with her daughter every day. She is beautiful and looks so kind, and he tells Dad they should get married. But Dad just laughs and says, "Life isn't a fairy tale, Mike! It isn't as simple as that!"
Mike would like to have a cat, too. But Dad says, "You know you are allergic to cats Mike, we can't..."
But tonight, just as they are sitting down in front of the TV screen, the doorbell rings.

D Answer the questions.

1. Two reasons Mike's dad is great: ....

....

2. a. Mike has ☐ a mom ☐ a brother ☐ a sister ☐ a dad ☐ a cat

b. Mike would like ☐ a mom ☐ a brother ☐ a sister ☐ a dad ☐ a cat

3. Choose the picture that corresponds to the story.

4. Mike's dad ☐ wants to get married ☐ doesn't want to get married.

Explain:..

Activity 2 Your Opinion

What do you think of Mike's life? Look at *Learn as You Wish* on the next page.

....

....

....

....

....

....

Learn as You Wish

Pour résumer ce que tu as appris sur Mike, choisis la méthode que tu préfères, A ou B.

A Remplis le tableau avec les informations que tu as apprises.

	What I know
Mike's relationship with his dad	
Mike's mom	
Family members	
Favourite ice cream	
Allergy?	
Present he wants for Christmas	
Present he made for his Dad	
His wishes for the future	

B Remplis les boîtes suivantes avec les informations que tu as apprises.

Present he made for his Dad

Mike's relationship with his dad

Favourite ice cream

Present he wants for Christmas

Family members

Allergy?

Mike's mom

His wishes for the future

Activity 3 Anticipation

But tonight, just as they are sitting down in front of the TV screen, the doorbell rings...

Ask your partner what he/she imagines is going to happen then write down what you think.

	My Partner	Me
Who's ringing the bell?		
Why?		
Good surprise ou bad surprise?		

Do you agree ?

Activity 4 Listening to the Next Part of the Story

MP3

A Listen and circle the right answer.

Who's standing at the door?			
What are they looking for?	a dog	a black cat	a grey cat
Mike and his Dad...	can help	cannot help	do not want to help
The people at the door leave...	a photo of the animal	their phone number	their address
That night Mike dreams of...			
When he wakes up, he sees...	a dog next to his bed	a cat next to his bed	a cat outside the window
Mike goes back to sleep...	with the dog next to his bed	with the cat next to his bed	with the cat in his bed
Mike's Dad...	sends a text message	phones someone	sends an email
Mike and his Dad are going to...	stay at home	take the animal to their neighbours	take the animal to the veterinarian

B Now sum up what happened.

But tonight, just as they are sitting down in front of the TV screen, the doorbell rings.

A .... and a .... are standing at the door.

They are looking for ....

....

....

....

....

Activity 5 Imagine the End of the Story

Imagine and write the end of the story. Look at the following picture and say how Mike's life has changed in one year.

....

....

....

....

....

....

....

....

Now read the end of the story on page 62.

December 24th, one year later

Your Task Write Mike's Diary

Write Mike's diary for December 24th, one year later.

Before you start, do you remember what Mike's wishes were?

He wanted ....

....

December 24th
Christmas Eve!

Last year, I

New Zealand's Wonders and Legends

Activity 1 Exchanging Information about New Zealand

A kiwi bird.

Pair A Do Activity 1 on this page.

Pair B Your Activity 1 is on page 63.

Maori art.

Pair A

A Complete the sentences with the followings words.

birds • youngest • kiwi • Maori

1. The .... are the indigenous people of New Zealand.

2. The .... is the national bird of New Zealand – a symbol of the country.

3. New Zealand has many colourful .... such as the tui and the pukeko.

4. First inhabited in the 13th century, New Zealand is called "the .... country" in the world.

B Prepare questions you can ask your partner to get extra information. If you need help, see Learn as You Wish.

1. New Zealand – weather? ....

2. A haka – what, origin? ....

3. Maori way of saying hello? ....

4. New Zealand's landscape? – monotonous? ....

C Ask your partner the questions and note their answers.

Learn as You Wish

Pour poser des questions, choisis la méthode que tu préfères, A ou B.

A Pour faire l'activité 1B, tu as besoin de certains des mots interrogatifs suivants.

What • How • Where • When • What is... like • Why • Who

B Pour faire l'activité 1B, tu as besoin de certaines des amorces de questions suivantes.

How do/does ... + BV? • What's ... like? • Who ...? • Is it ...? • Can you name ...? • What about ...? • What do they look like? • What ...? • When did ...?

Activity 2 Telling a Legend

A **Can you reconstruct the legend? This is how the Maori say New Zealand was created. Put the following words in the right order.**

a giant fish | was pulled from | a legend | says | the ocean | this land | like

B **Draw a picture to illustrate the legend and find a title for it.**

C **1. Get ready to retell the legend.**
You are Maori storytellers. Write your own version of the legend. Use the following prompts and don't forget to include descriptions.

A Maori legend explains ....

First, there was only the ocean. It was ....

There wasn't .... just ....

But one day the ocean became.. and a new land ....

The land is ....

2. Here are a few elements you can use to complete the legend. You have to make your choice and reorder them of course.

any land • any sky • black • came out of the huge waves • dark blue • emerged from the water • how New Zealand was created • water • New Zealand • our country • powerful and violent • the creation of New Zealand • agitated • transparent • water everywhere

Activity 3 The Kiwi: A Legend

A **1. Label the pictures with the following words:**

a forest • the sky • a tree • wings • a nest • legs • the ground

2. The kiwi bird before and now. Imagine the reasons.

....

....

....

....

Before Now

3. Now listen to the legend.

4. Find the words corresponding to the phonetics. Practise their pronunciation.

wings • bird • tree • guardian • ground • Maori

a. /ˈmaʊrɪ/ ....

b. /ˈgɑːdɪən/ ....

c. /triː/ ....

d. /bɜːd/ ....

e. /wɪŋz/ ....

f. /graʊnd/ ....

B **Now listen to the legend again. Read the sentences and match each one to the corresponding picture.**

a. Bugs are attacking the trees.
b. Kiwi is now a symbol of N.Z., because he's the bravest of birds.
c. Many birds refuse to help because they're scared.
d. Tanemahuta, the Guardian of the Forest, asks the birds for help.
e. Kiwi agrees to help and kills all the bugs.

C True or False? Write "true" for the true statements. Cross out the mistaken information and correct it for the ones that are false.

1. The Guardian of the Forest needs help. ....
2. His brother is the Guardian of the Sea. ....
3. The trees in the forest are in great danger. ....
4. The birds live on the clouds in the sky. ....
5. One bird must sacrifice himself to save the trees. ....

MP3

D 1. Listen and pronounce these words out loud. Is the stress on the first or second syllable?

Maori • guardian • forest • brother • attack • abandon • afraid • another • generous • beautiful • famous • symbol

Stress on the first syllable	Stress on the second syllable

2. What can you conclude about the schwa, the /ə/ sound as in "afraid" /əˈfreɪd/? Underline the correct answer.

In English /ə/ is mainly found in stressed / unstressed syllables.

Your Task Mime the Story

You are going to act out the story without speaking, but you can show the audience some title cards with the characters' words or a short sentence to explain the situation.

Step 1. The "actors".

Bugs. How many: ....

Who: ....

The kiwi. Who: ....

Birds. How many: ....

Who: ....

Tanemahuta, the Guardian of the Forest.

Who : ....

Step 2. How do you show the following actions or feelings? Mime them.

attacking • being brave • refusing to help • being scared • asking for help • agreeing to help • killing the bugs

Step 3. What title cards are you going to write?

One of you must abandon your wings.

Step 4. Practise until you think you are ready to perform in front of the class or to make a video of your performance.

Kruger Park Safari

Activity 1 Are There Any Lions?

A **To get ready for a safari, look at the map and the webpage. Where is Kruger Park?**

B **Get ready to role-play a telephone conversation**

Pupil A **Your instructions are on this page.**
Pupil B **Your instructions are on the next page.**

Pupil A
You are Ann or Peter McGregor, a British tourist, and you are going to Kruger Park, in South Africa for a safari. You phone your travel agent to get some practical information before leaving. Ask about:
- The Big Five: elephants, lions, buffaloes, rhinos, leopards
- Clothes (cold at night?)
- Equipment (camera, binoculars, cell phone, sunglasses ...)

Use: Are there any ... in the park? • Is it easy to see ... in the park? • What equipment ... do I need? • Is it usually ... during the day / at night? • Can I see ... at night?

TIPS
MP3 *Écoute les noms d'animaux et entraîne-toi à les prononcer.*

Pupil B

You are Helen, the travel agent, and you use the information below to answer the questions.

Use : No there aren't ... • Yes, there is ... • Yes, you can see ... • No, you can't ... • You must ... • Yes, there are ... in the park • No, there aren't any.

TIPS

MP3 *Écoute les noms d'animaux et entraîne-toi à les prononcer.*

Kruger Park safaris: information for tourists					
Animals	**Elephants:** common (every day)	**Lions :** common (at night)	**Buffaloes:** very common	**Rhinos:** rare (endangered species)	**Leopards:** not very common (early morning)
Weather	Hot during the day / can be cool at night				
Equipment	Binoculars available at the park. Do not forget: camera, sunglasses, cell phone.				

Activity 2 On Safari in Kruger Park

MP3

A Listen to the recording.

What animals did the McGregors see? Tick the right boxes.

B Are the McGregors happy? ☐ Yes ☐ No

Circle the adjectives you hear that justify your answer:

marvellous • scary • wonderful • dangerous • cool • fantastic • boring • great • amazing • ugly • beautiful • fabulous

Learn as You Wish

Pour organiser ce que tu as appris, relis pages 33 et 34 et choisis la méthode que tu préfères, A ou B.

A

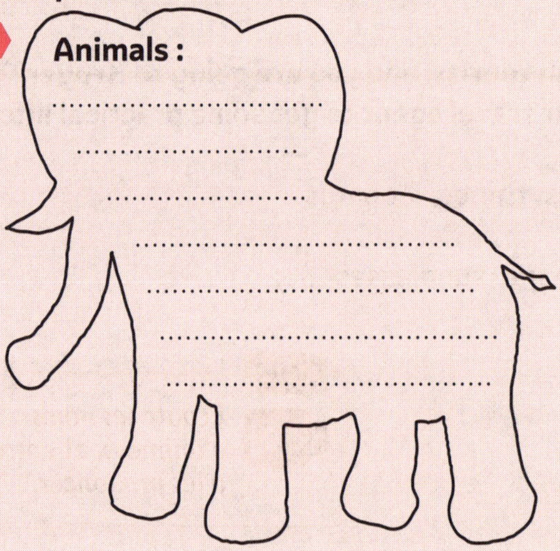

B

Your Task Write a Postcard

Complete the postcard the McGregors wrote to Helen.

Dear Helen,

We are at Kruger Park. There are a lot of .... everywhere.

Today we went on a .... trip!

We saw some .... with a cute .... one, a ...., a .... and .... rhinos.

We saw a beautiful .... but .... are not one of the Big Five. Unfortunately, there was no .... so we only saw .... big animals. But Kruger Park is really ....!!!

Thank you for your help and your advice.

Learn as You Wish

Pour résumer, choisis, A, B ou C.

A I'd really love to visit Kruger Park because ....

....

....

....

B My favourite Big Five animal is

...................., because it is ....

and .... It is easy to see

it .... but you have to

....

@ CONNECT TO: collegien.nathan.fr/speak6

C The McGregors are really lucky! They went to Kruger Park to

....

....

and they saw ....

....

The only problem was that

....

But, they were ...., especially the children.

Utilise ce que tu as appris dans les activités 1 et 2.

Be My Valentine

Activity 1 Celebrations

A **What celebrations are these cards for? Write the correct celebration under each card.**

Christmas • Mother's Day • Father's Day • Halloween

B **What do you do for these celebrations? Complete the sentences.**

make cards for my friends • make a card for my father • make a card for my mother • wear costumes and masks • decorate the house with green, gold and red lights • buy a Christmas tree • decorate the house with pumpkins • go trick or treating • eat sweets and chocolate • buy presents and gifts • receive presents

1. For Christmas, ……………………………………
2. For Mother's Day, ……………………………………
3. For Father's Day, ……………………………………
4. For Halloween, I ……………………………………

C 1. Cross out the presents people don't give or don't receive on Valentine's Day.

2. Complete the sentence using "give" or "receive".

a. For Valentine's Day, people don't ....

b. For Valentine's Day, people ....

Activity 2 Celebration Names and Dates

A 1. Complete with the correct month of the year.

a. It is the twelfth month of the year. ....

b. The second month of the year is called ....

c. Halloween is on the last day of ...., the tenth month of the year.

d. My birthday is in ....

2. Complete with the appropriate ordinal number (first, fourth ...).

a. February is the .... month of the year.

b. Christmas is on December the ....

c. On the .... of October, I wear a costume and celebrate Halloween.

d. My birthday is on ....

Learn as You Wish

Pour apprendre les mots nouveaux, choisis la méthode que tu préfères, A ou B :

A Recopie les mots nouveaux et fais un dessin ou colle une photo pour t'en souvenir.

Exemple :
gift

B Fais une phrase pour réemployer les mots nouveaux.

....

....

....

TIPS

MP3 *N'oublie pas d'écouter les mots enregistrés. Répète-les plusieurs fois.*

B **Choose the correct names and dates of the celebrations, and write the colours associated with them.**

Valentine's Day • Christmas • Halloween • 31st October • 14th February • 25th December

1.

Trick or Treat!

Name: ....

Date: ....

Colour(s): ....

2.

Name: ....

Date: ....

Colour(s): ....

Santa Claus

3.

Sweetheart

Name: ....

Date: ....

Colour(s): ....

Learn as You Wish

Des acrostiches sont des poèmes autour d'un mot. Voici deux exemples :

Love is a beautiful thing.
On
Valentine's Day
Everyone is loved.

Beautifu**L** feelings
Marvell**O**us moments
Hea**V**en on earth
Grac**E** and happiness

Pour rédiger un acrostiche, choisis l'activité que tu préfères, A (un mot très court) ou B (un mot plus long). Aide-toi des mots dans le nuage ci-dessous.

A Love • Heart • Friend

B Girlfriend • Boyfriend • Friendship

fabulous handsome sweet gentle dearest generous free love romantic music passion rose angel sky pretty respect star fun happy dear fascinating great affection laugh together beauty dance honey smile game emotion gently declare everyone garden heart darling perfect peace kindness moon light forever ideal relationship appreciate charming

Activity 3 "Be My Valentine" Song

MP3 **Listen to the song and complete the text.**

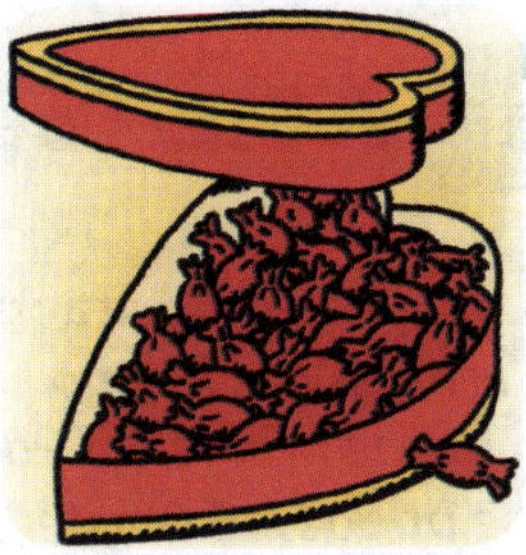

A box of ....

in a big red ....

I will send it with all my love.

CHORUS
Will you be ....?
Will you love me all the time?
How will I know your love is true?
When will you say to me - I love you?

A bunch of ....

in a big ....
You sent it to me with all your love.
With all your love.

Words
- bunch (n) *bouquet*
- send, sent (v) *envoyer*
- true (adj) *vrai(e)*

CHORUS
Will you be ....?
Will you love me all the time?
How will I know your love is true?

Your Task Write a Celebration Card

Draw your own card, colour it and write 4 short lines.

Who is your card for?:
brother • mother/Mum • sister • friend • pet • teacher • father/Dad

Example: *This card is for my Mum, Ann. This card is for my friend Mark.*

Which celebration is your card for?

This card is for ....
Happy ....
....
....
....
....
Love ....

Towns and Cities

Activity 1 A City Poem

Listen to the poem and practise saying it.

The bridges of Chicago
are not the bridges of Paris
or the bridges of Amsterdam...

Jerome Rothenberg, "The Chicago Poem", 1931

Activity 2 Cities and Landmarks

Try to match a photo of a landmark and a city. Choose to do A or B.

A

• Sydney • Dublin • London • New York

B

• London • Chicago • Edinburgh • San Francisco

Which landmarks can you name?

Picture ☐ is....................................... .

It's in ....

I don't know the name of the landmark in picture ☐

but it must be in ....

TIPS

Essaie de faire des hypothèses, même si tu n'es pas certain(e).

Activity 3 City Skylines

Match the skyline and the city it belongs to and exchange with your partner.

Sydney • New York • London • Chicago • Edinburgh

1. ....

2. ....

3. ....

4. ....

5. ....

I think number one is .... because I can see ....

I'm not sure but I think it's .... because ....

....

I think .... is .... in ....

but I'm not quite sure. Can you help me? What do you think?

I think • Do you agree? • I'm not sure. Can you help me? • I don't know. Do you? • I don't recognise this city. • I don't agree. • I don't think it is ...

Activity 4 About the Cities

A Read these texts to find the missing information. Don't try to understand every word.

Edinburgh's most popular and famous attraction, Edinburgh Castle dominates the city skyline. It was home to royalty for hundreds of years including Queen Margaret, Mary Queen of Scots and James VI. Today, it is a military fort.

Willis Tower is one of North America's tallest buildings. It is home to large, well-known companies. More than an office building, it's a cultural landmark and iconic Chicago tourist attraction.

On 26th January each year, Australians come together to celebrate their national day. Two free concerts for all ages are staged at the Sydney Opera House on Australia Day.

The London Eye stands 135 metres high near Westminster Bridge. It is the world's highest observation wheel. You can get panoramic views of Big Ben and the Houses of Parliament, the Tower of London and Tower Bridge on the River Thames.

Located in New York Harbor, the Statue of Liberty was a gift of friendship from the people of France to the United States in 1886. It is recognised as a universal symbol of freedom and democracy.

B What did you learn?

I learnt that .... is in ....

Now I know that ....

C Go back to Activity 3 with your partner and confirm your guesses. Report to your class.

Activity 5 My City: Liverpool

Faye is from Liverpool. Listen to her talk about her city.

A Listen to Part 1 and answer the question:

1. What nationality is Faye? ....

2. Can you find Liverpool on this map?

3. Liverpool is in
☐ the west
☐ the east of ....

4. Try to find more information about Liverpool:

1

2

3

4

a. Which picture is not one of Faye's favourite places in Liverpool? ....

b. Can you guess which picture is:

The Albert Dock? ....

Crosby Beach? ....

The Liver Building? ....

c. What can you say about the Liver Building?

It's the .... of Liverpool

d. Did you hear an example of art? ....

B Now listen to Part 2.

1. Tick the right box:

☐ If you like history, Liverpool is for you.
☐ If you like history, Liverpool is not for you.
So, what can you say about Liverpool? Liverpool is a very .... city.

☐ If you like music, Liverpool is for you.
☐ If you like music, Liverpool is not for you.
So, what can you say about Liverpool? Liverpool is a very .... city.

Did you hear an example of a band? ....

2. Other activities for visitors to Liverpool: ....

C **Let's recap. Tick the right boxes (☑) then copy the recap below.**

Liverpool is a very ☐ boring ☐ interesting ☐ artistic ☐ ugly ☐ musical ☐ new ☐ historical city.
It's Faye's .... city because she thinks it's ☐ enormous ☐ not too big and it's full of ☐ ordinary ☐ exciting places for visitors.
She loves ☐ sleeping ☐ walking on Crosby Beach and watching the ☐ boats ☐ birds ☐ statues. She thinks it's a .... city!

....

....

....

....

....

Activity 6 Acrostic Poem

A **Look at this acrostic poem about Paris. Listen to the poem and practise saying it:**

Pretty
Artistic
Radiant
Interesting
Superb

B **Now, choose a city:**

London • New York • Sydney • Chicago • Liverpool • Edinburgh

Pick out words from the lists below and write your own acrostic poem about the city of your choice.

☺ artistic • attractive • beautiful • changing • dynamic • elegant • enormous • great • ideal • interesting • kaleidoscopic • kind • laughing • lovely • neighbourly • nice • only one • open • panoramic • pretty • proud • radiant • safe • sailing • splendid • superb • surfing • world-famous • yummy • young

☹ big • boring • cloudy • cold • noisy • rainy • sleepy • speedy • upsetting • wet • worrying

C **Practise saying your poem and get ready to perform in front of the class.**

TIPS
Rappelle-toi que l'anglais est musical et que tu peux faire des gestes.

Activity 7 In the Town

MP3 **A** **Circle the places you hear.**

school

church

park

swimming pool

cinema

supermarket

bookshop

recycling centre

bank

town hall

museum

bench

fountain

ice cream vendor

icerink

flower bed

B **Now practise saying the words.**

Activity 8 Your Town

A Make a map!
Create your own picture of the land around your school.
Name the streets.
Identify the buildings and green spaces, and the places you think are important.

B What are your favourite places in your hometown?

....

....

C Are there any works of art in your hometown?

There's ....

I like / I don't like / My favourite is ....

statue • graffiti • mural • optical illusion

Learn as You Wish

Pour retenir le vocabulaire de la ville, choisis la méthode que tu préfères, A ou B.

A

Town/City

- Good points: *exciting ...*
- Bad points: *boring ...*
- Equipment: *fountain ...*
- Places in the city: *museum ...*

B **Crée un livre d'images pour enfants : dessine un bâtiment, un équipement, une décoration et écris son nom à côté du dessin.**

Exemple : *bench*

Activity 9 Changes to the City

A **Do you remember Faye? Listen to what she says about Liverpool. What are the differences between Liverpool in the past and Liverpool now? Tick the boxes.**

1. In the past there ☐ was lots to do ☐ wasn't very much to do.
2. Now there ☐ is a lot to do ☐ isn't a lot to do.
3. In the past there ☐ were many shops ☐ weren't many shops.
4. Now there ☐ are many shops ☐ aren't many shops.
5. In the past Liverpool ☐ wasn't a boring city ☐ was a boring city.
6. Now Liverpool ☐ isn't an exciting city ☐ is an exciting city.

B **Listen and find something Faye really likes in modern Liverpool:** ....

Now find something she doesn't like. She thinks Liverpool is too ....
She'd like the city to be ☐ bigger ☐ cleaner ☐ warmer ☐ more artistic.

C **What about your hometown? Would you like some changes? First add things you'd like to see on your map. Then write what you'd like.**

I'd like a .... near the ....

....

Your Task Write a Manifesto

Write a manifesto to make the space around your school a better place for young people. First identify the problems, then suggest solutions.

A **Match the problem and the solution.**

Problem	Idea
There are no public spaces for us.	We need car-free streets.
The streets are dangerous.	We want trees, pools and fountains everywhere.
There is no space for nature in the city.	We want play areas for young people.

B **Find more problems and solutions.**

C **Write a manifesto.**

Learn as You Wish

Pour parler d'une ville, choisis la méthode que tu préfères, A ou B.

A Tu peux prendre le rôle de Faye et présenter oralement Liverpool.

B Tu peux présenter oralement ta ville en t'inspirant de Faye.

TIPS
N'oublie pas de t'exercer à dire tes revendications.

Who Is It?

Activity 1 Who Are They?

A **Who are these people? Write the correct name under each photo.**

Queen Elizabeth II • David Cameron • Adele • Daniel Radcliffe

B **You are going to play a game to guess a mystery character. Write the questions you need to ask.**

1. man/woman:

2. young/elderly person:

3. dead/alive:

4. nationality (English, American...) :

5. job (singer, actor...) :

C **Now, answer the questions for one of the people in the photos.**

Activity 2 Who Is It?

MP3

A Listen to Part 1. Who is playing the game? Tick the correct answer.

☐ **1.** Three elderly people.
☐ **2.** A doctor and a patient.
☐ **3.** An adult and two children.

B Listen again.

1. Tick the right boxes.

2. Write the words you hear that correspond to each illustration

	☐ Yes ☐ No	☐ Yes ☐ No	☐ Yes ☐ No	☐ Yes ☐ No	☐ Yes ☐ No	
Words:	Words:	Words:	Words:	Words:	Words:	Words: ....

Learn as You Wish

Pour récapituler les informations que tu as trouvées sur le personnage mystère, choisis l'activité que tu préfères, A ou B.

A À partir de l'activité 2, complète les phrases suivantes : entoure les mots qui conviennent et écris les mots qui correspondent aux images.

I know that the mystery character is .... 

He/she is/isn't ....  He/she is/isn't .... 

He/she is/isn't ....  His/her songs/films are ....  

He/she is .... 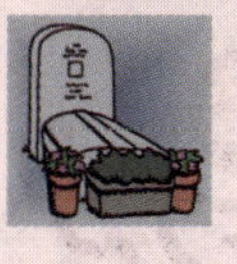

B À partir de l'activité 2, écris un paragraphe sur le personnage mystère.

....

....

....

MP3 **C** **Listen to Part 2. Circle the objects you hear.**

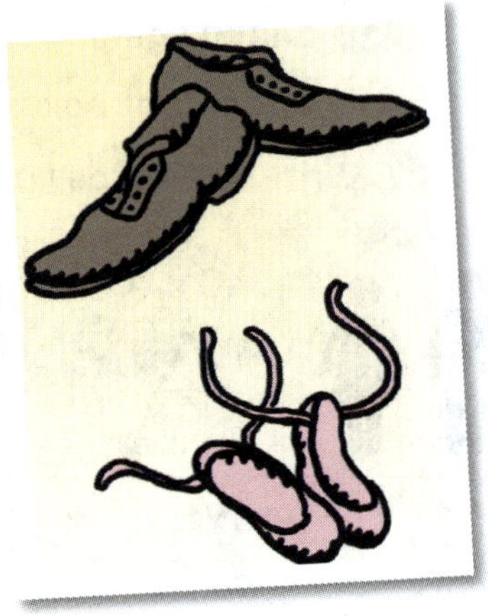

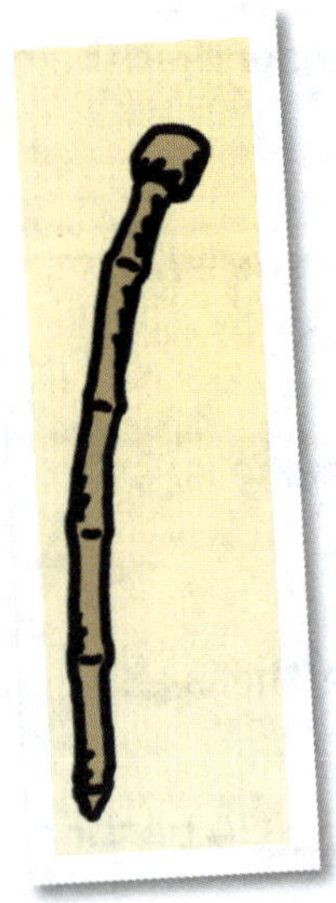

Do you know who the mystery character is ? ....

Activity 3 Celebrity Webquest

@ CONNECT TO: collegien.nathan.fr/speak6

A Get ready for Your Task. Look on the website for the celebrity your teacher gives you. Click on the photo and read the "Quick Facts" and "Best Known for" sections to take notes:

	The personality I chose	The personality my partner chose
Gender (female or male)		
Dead or alive (dates)		
Job		
Age (young, middle-aged, elderly)		
Physical characteristics		
Famous for		

MP3

B Practise asking questions: listen and repeat the questions, paying attention to the rhythm.

Your Task Role-play a "Who Is It?" Game

A Work in pairs.

1. Pupil A. Ask your partner questions about her/his celebrity from Activity 3.
When you think you know who the celebrity is, stop asking questions and recap orally what you know about him or her (go back to p. 49 for help).

Pupil B. Answer your partner's questions.
Use short answers only. Do not give away the name of your celebrity.

2. Change roles.

3. Write a paragraph about the celebrity your partner chose.

....

....

B Teamwork Competition

In teams, choose four famous people and answer the other team's questions. Change roles.

You will score: 1 point for a precise and correct answer.
1 point for a correct question.
1 point for recapping before guessing the name.
2 points if you ask a question to check your guess.

Iluq, an Inuit Boy

Activity 1 Inuit Culture

A The Inuit are indigenous people who live in the Arctic, in Canada, Alaska (U.S.A.) and Greenland.

Inuit children wearing traditional fur parkas. It is very cold in the Arctic!

Inuit traditionally used dog sleds for transport.

Today, they also use snowmobiles.

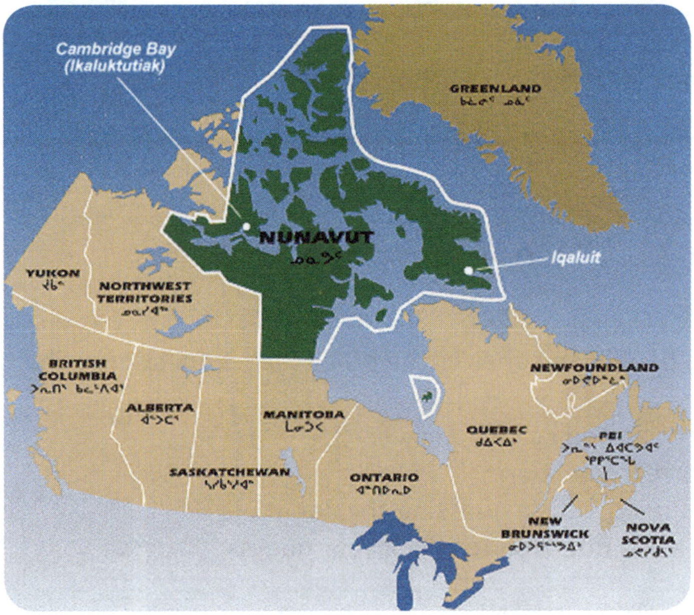

In Canada, many Inuit live in a vast territory called Nunavut.

B **Match each Inuit object to its equivalent in your country. Look out! One picture doesn't have a pair.**

an igloo

a caribou

a sled

ice skates

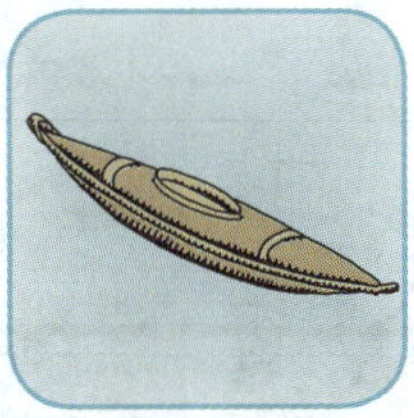
a kayak

a walrus

a snowmobile

a cow

a house

rollerblades

a car

a scooter

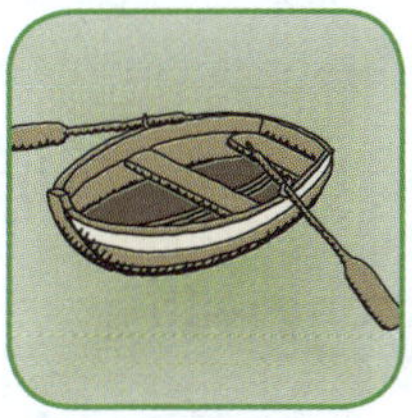
a rowing boat

Activity 2 Vocabulary Crossword

Complete the crossword.

Across

3. A quiet animal that lives in the Far North. The Inuit eat its meat.

6. A quiet animal that gives milk.

9. Shoes that have wheels.

10. You can .... on the ice.

Down

1. An Inuit boat.

2. Do you live in an apartment or a ....?

4. A house made of ice.

5. It has two wheels and an engine.

7. An animal that can swim in the water and move on the ground. It has two very long teeth.

8. What do you use to cross a lake?

Activity 3 Iluq and his Family Today

A Iluq lives in Nunavut, Canada. Look at the pictures and complete the paragraph with words in the box.

father • mother • brother • friends • snowmobile • small house • dad

I ride a .... to school.

I live in a .... I have a .... and a sister. My .... is a fisherman and my .... is a schoolteacher!

In winter I go skating with my ....

In the summer I go fishing with my sister and my ....

B You can listen to Iluq's story to check your answers.

Activity 4 Iluq's Family in the Past

Look at the pictures, read the story, then write the number of the picture in front of the corresponding sentence in the story.

A long time ago... My grandpa's name was Apoutsiak (Little Snowflake). ☐ He had a sled and five dogs. In winter it was cold outside! ☐ My grandpa and my grandma used snow and ice to make an igloo. ☐ They lived in it... and it was warm inside! Nights were very, very long. ☐ In summer, my grandpa and my grandma went fishing on their kayak. And they lived on the kayak; days were very, very long!

Activity 5 Summarising

Recap everything you know about Inuit people.

Regions where they live: ....

Climate: ....

Housing in the past: ....

Housing in the present: ....

Familiar activities in the past: ....

Familiar activities today: ....

Your Task A Phone Conversation with Iluq

Iluq is going to talk to his French penfriend on the phone.

Pupil A, you are Iluq.

Pupil B, you play yourself, the penfriend.

See Learn as You Wish on page 56 for help preparing the conversation.

Learn as You Wish

Pour préparer ton dialogue, choisis la méthode que tu préfères, A ou B. Réutilise ce que tu as appris sur les Inuits, et répète le dialogue jusqu'à ce que tu sois à l'aise.

A Si tu le souhaites, utilise les suggestions suivantes pour commencer à construire ton dialogue.

Penfriend: start the conversation / say who you are...

Iluq: you're happy / your first question is about the place of residence...

Penfriend: your answer (residence / city / what you like about it) + a question...

Iluq: your answer (where you live now / where your grandparents lived) + question about the weather...

Penfriend: answer + question about the weather...

B Les amorces suivantes vont t'aider à dialoguer. Complète les questions et les réponses, puis rajoutes-en.

Penfriend: Hello .... This is ...., I'm your penfriend from ....

Iluq: Hey, great to hear your voice! I want to know everything about you, but first of all ....?

Penfriend: I live in a house/apartment/........................... in ....

I like it because .... And what about you?

Iluq: My grandparents lived in an .... but now I live in a .... with my parents, it's more .... Hey, what's the weather like today in France?

Penfriend: Oh, it's not too .... Is it cold in your country right now?

Iluq: ....

Penfriend: That must be terrible! You can't do anything when it's so ....!

Iluq: Oh, no, I love it, we can ....!

St Patrick's Day Soda Bread

Activity 1 St Patrick's Day

A **Read the text.**

St Patrick's Day, the Irish national day, is March 17th.

Everyone wears green, the colour of Ireland. There is a big parade in Dublin, with Irish music and dancing. And people eat special green food: green cake, green cheese…! St Patrick's Day is also celebrated in other countries where people of Irish origin live: particularly Australia and the USA.

On St Patrick's Day, you can see lots of Irish flags and shamrocks – green plants with three leaves that are considered lucky.

These Irish dancers have beautiful costumes with Celtic designs.

The leprechaun – a small, magical man who has a treasure – is another traditional symbol of Ireland.

B **Irish people eat green food and drink green drinks on St Patrick's Day. Circle the four things that are NOT green.**

lemons – courgettes – carrots – lettuce – broccoli

kiwi fruit – pistachio ice-cream – avocadoes – coffee

Brussels sprouts – ketchup – cucumbers – mint tea

Activity 2 Listening to a Recipe for St Patrick's Day

You can make soda bread, an Irish speciality, for St Patrick's Day.

MP3 **A These are the ingredients. Listen and repeat each word.**

flour • salt • baking powder • bicarbonate • milk • vinegar • raisins • food colouring

MP3 **B Listen to the recipe and number the pictures in the right order.**

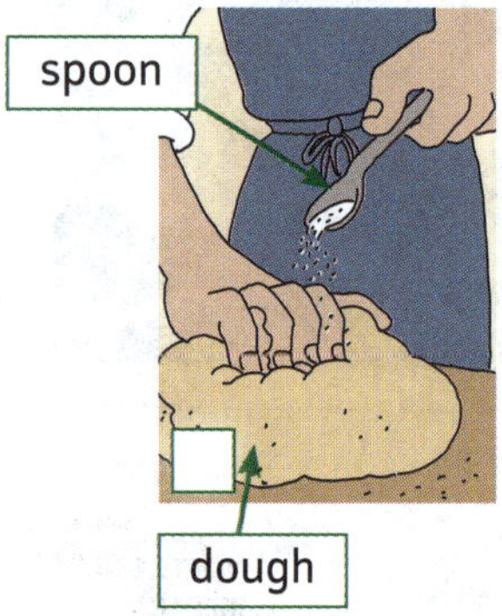

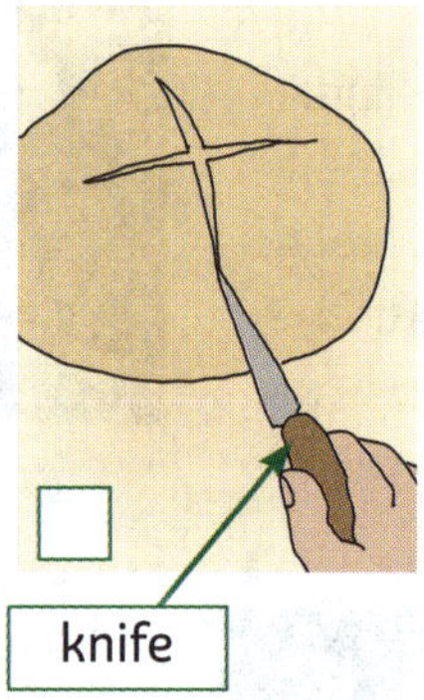

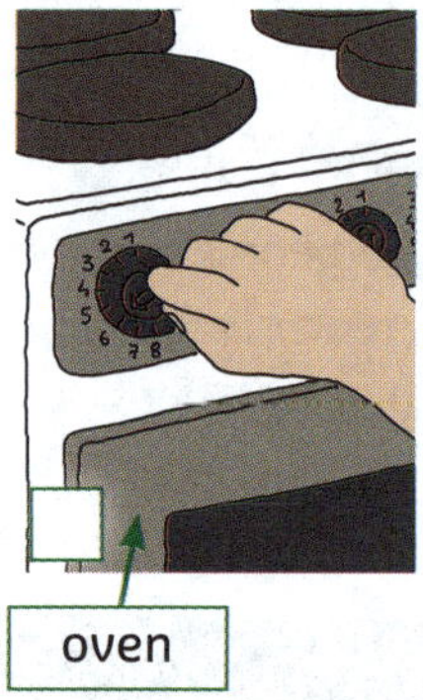

C Listen to the recipe again. Circle the numbers you hear.

1/2	1	2	3	4
5	6	7	8	9
10	14	15	20	30
40	50	80	100	150
190	200	250	290	300

D Now, listen to the first part again and write out the ingredients and their quantities.

.... grams ....

.... tablespoon ....

.... (or ....)

.... millilitres ....

.... teaspoon ....

Optional: ....

....

Activity 3 Making Soda Bread

Try to match each verb to the rest of its sentence. Then listen to the recipe again to check.

1. Turn	**a.** the flour, baking powder and salt.
2. Add	**b.** it in the oven for 30 to 40 minutes.
3. Mix	**c.** it on the day you make it.
4. Press	**d.** the oven on to 190°.
5. Cut	**e.** a cross into the top with a knife.
6. Bake	**f.** the vinegar to the milk.
7. Eat	**g.** the dough on the table with your hands.

Activity 4 Pronunciation

MP3

A Listen and repeat the following words:

enough • flour • ball • dough • powder • bowl • colouring • oven • salt • slowly • buttered

B Now sort the words into the table by pronunciation.

/aʊ/ (now)	/ʌ/ (Dublin)	/əʊ/ (go)	/ɔː/ (all)

C Listen to instruction n°5 and repeat it as many times as you want: you should sound English!

Record yourself. Listen to yourself and make sure you sound as close as possible to the English-speaking person.

Activity 5 Recipe Language

A With a partner, reread Activities 1-4. Note as many words as possible in the circles.

I eat with

What I put food or drinks in

Cake recipe ingredients

B Fill in the blanks with *How much?* or *How many?*

1. .... grams of flour did you say?

2. .... salt did you say?

3. .... milk did you say?

4. .... tablespoons of salt did you say?

5. .... bicarbonate powder did you say?

Your Task Record a Recipe

Record (audio or, even better, video) a traditional British or American recipe or your favourite dish. You do not have to really make the recipe, you can only explain how to make it or mime what you are supposed to do.

@ CONNECT TO: collegien.nathan.fr/speak6 **to see videos of young English-speaking people, and a famous chef, presenting recipes.**

First, write down the list of ingredients and the quantities:

....

....

....

....

Then write the recipe as a list of simple instructions

....

....

....

....

....

Remember:

- Add elements that will make your recipe interesting (when people eat it, why you chose it, if it is easy or difficult.
- Before you record yourself, think about the audience. They will take notes so speak slowly and loudly.

Look at the evaluation sheet below. The audience is going to use it to assess your presentation.

Presenting a Recipe

	Recipe 1	Recipe 2	Recipe 3	Recipe 4	Recipe 5
The ingredients were presented clearly.	☐	☐	☐	☐	☐
The difficult words were explained.	☐	☐	☐	☐	☐
It was easy to take notes.	☐	☐	☐	☐	☐
I have enough elements to make the recipe alone.	☐	☐	☐	☐	☐
The tone was varied and enthusiastic.	☐	☐	☐	☐	☐
The voice was clear / loud enough.	☐	☐	☐	☐	☐
The recipe was "acted" and not read.	☐	☐	☐	☐	☐
It was easy to follow.	☐	☐	☐	☐	☐

Activity 3 Identifying a Suspect

Pupil B

A **You are going to role play a witness who saw a strange man near the Parliament. Prepare by writing the words in the correct boxes on the illustrations and tick the correct adjectives.**

shoes • a jacket • a torch • a barrel • a beard • a moustache • a cape • boots • a hat • a sword

TIPS

MP3 *Écoute les mots et entraîne-toi à les prononcer.*

B **You saw a strange man near the Parliament. Select the person you saw and answer your partner's questions with short answers.**

TIPS

Yes, he was…

I'm absolutely positive…

Yes, I think he was…

I'm not so sure any more.

Yes, it seems to me that … but it was dark.

White Christmas – Part 4

A **Read the end of the story.**

December 24th One Year Later

Mike is sitting on the sofa watching Avatar with Carol. Kitty is sleeping on Mike's lap. There are plenty of presents with nice red ribbons at the foot of the Christmas tree. In the kitchen, Dad is carving the turkey and Sheryl is taking a cake out of the oven. Mike's aunt and uncle and cousins are arriving in half an hour. And then they will open the presents!

This is their last Christmas in this house. Mike and his dad, and Carol and her mom, are all moving to a new bigger house. Carol and Mike have a new baby brother. And luckily, Mike isn't allergic to cats any more!

B **Is the end similar to your version?**

The Simpsons, America's First Family

Activity 3. Pupil B

B **Read the description and guess who the character is:**

She is eight years old, and she has an older brother and a younger sister. She is short with spiky hair and she always wears a red dress. She is very smart and ambitious. She finds her brother very annoying because he is so immature! She loves reading and playing the saxophone.

Her name is: ....

C **Prepare questions to help you find out who your partner's character is. Ask about the character's:**

a. Looks?
b. Age?
c. Family?
d. Personality?
e. Likes and dislikes?
f. Hobbies?

Activity 1 Exchanging Information about New Zealand

Pupil B

A Complete the sentences with the following words.

nose and forehead • mild • haka • forests

Saying "hello" with a hongi.

A Maori haka dance.

New Zealand's mountain landscape.

1. A .... is a traditional dance of the Maori people of New Zealand. It was originally performed by warriors before a battle to intimidate the opponent.

2. New Zealand has a .... climate.

3. Hongi is a traditional Maori greeting: pressing your .... onto the other person's face when meeting.

4. New Zealand has a diverse landscape with amazing mountains, beaches and green ....

B Prepare questions you will ask your partner to get extra information. If you need help, see Learn as You Wish, page 29.

1. First inhabitants of New Zealand – When?

....

2. New Zealand's birds – Some names? Particularity?

....

3. The kiwi ? ....

4. Indigenous people of New Zealand?

....

C Ask your partner the questions and note their answers.

Crédits photographiques

4 CHRISTOPHE L COLLECTION ; **5 bg mg md bd hd** CHRISTOPHE L COLLECTION ; **8** CHRISTOPHE L COLLECTION ; **12 hg bg** Britainonview **12 md** AFP / LEON NEAL ; **16 h** SHUTTERSTOCK/ruidoblanco ; **16 mh1** SHUTTERSTOCK/ Tim UR ; **16 mh2** SHUTTERSTOCK/ Timmary ; **16 mh3** 123RF/Bogdan Ionescu ; **16 mh4** FOTOLIA/Nadger ; **16 mh5** SHUTTERSTOCK/P. Brighton ; **16 mb6** SHUTTERSTOCK/J. Gough ; **16 mb7** SHUTTERSTOCK/Tobic ; **16 mb8** SHUTTERSTOCK/JIRI HERA ; **16 mb9** 123RF/Gresei ; **17 h1** 123RF/G. Tsartsianidis ; **17 h2** SHUTTERSTOCK/I. Behrens-Kunkel ; **17 h3** SHUTTERSTOCK/ Subjus ; **17 h4** SHUTTERSTOCK/Dancake ; **17 h5** FOTOLIA/Posteriori ; **17 h6** 123R/A. Ignatenco ; **17 h7** 123RF/L. Borysovskyi ; **17 h8** SHUTTERSTOCK/Fatseyeva ; **17 h9** 123RF/M. Blach ; **17 h10** 123RF/ Chode ; **17 h11** 123RF/V.Sheppella ; **17 h12** 123R/S. Rahunoks ; **17 h13** SHUTTERSTOCK/Dancake ; **19 h1 md2** SHUTTERSTOCK/Gts ; **19 h2 mg3** SHUTTERSTOCK/VictoriaKh ; **19 h3 mg2** SHUTTERSTOCK/L. Molinero ; **19 h4 bg3** iStock/Floortje ; **19 h5 mg1** 123RF/G. Tsartsianidis ; 19 md1 123RF/O. Trakevych ; **19 bg1** SHUTTERSTOCK/Dancake ; **19 bg2** SHUTTERSTOCK/K. Usata ; **19 bd1** 123RF/J. Aunion ; **19 bd2** 123RF/G. Tsartsianidis ; **19 bd3** iStock/Dusty Pixel ; **19 bd4** iStock/Arsela ; **19 bd5** SHUTTERSTOCK/P. Suwannaket ; **19 bd6** 123RF/D. Koltovskyi ; **20 hg1** SHUTTERSTOCK/Tobic ; **20 h2** SHUTTERSTOCK/Jiri Hera ; **20 h3** SHUTTERSTOCK/ Timmary ; **20 hd4** SHUTTERSTOCK/ Tim UR ; **20 mg1** SHUTTERSTOCK/ ruidoblanco ; **20 m2** SHUTTERSTOCK/Ingvar Bjork ; **20 md3** SHUTTERSTOCK/P. Suwannaket ; **20 mg4** SHUTTERSTOCK/Paul_Brighton ; **20 m5** SHUTTERSTOCK/VictoriaKh ; **20 m6** SHUTTERSTOCK/Ines Behrens-Kunkel ; **20 md7** 123RF Limited/Handmadepictures ; **20 bg1** 123RF Limited/Bogdan Ionescu ; **20 b2** SHUTTERSTOCK/K. Usata ; **20 bd3** FOTOLIA/Nadger ; **21 mg** FOTOLIA/MSPPHOTOGRAPHIC ; **21 m** SHUTTERSTOCK/Hurst Photo ; **21 md** SHUTTERSTOCK/Brian C. Weed **21 b** SHUTTERSTOCK/ Nikolayenko Yekaterina ; **22 hg1** SHUTTERSTOCK/ Tim UR ; **22 h2** 123RF/L. Borysovskyi ; **22 h3** 123R/A. Ignatenco ; **22 hd4** 123RF Limited/Bogdan Ionescu ; **22 mg1** 123RF/Gresei ; **22 m2** SHUTTERSTOCK/ Fatseyeva ; **22 m3** 123RF/M. Blach ; **22 md4** 123RF/Chode ; **22 bg1** FOTOLIA/Posteriori ; **23** Stockbyte **24** THINKSTOCK / HannamariaH THINKSTOCK ; **29 h b** New Zealand Tourism ; **33** South African Tourism ; **36 h g** THINKSTOCK/Brand X Pictures **h m** City of Chicago **h d** Dust | Dreamstime.com **b** THINKSTOCK / amiloslava ; **37 b** Visitbritain; **40 hg1** Visitbritain ; **40 h2** Marley White / NYC&Co ; **40 h3** Ethan Rohloff / Destination New South Wales ; **40 hd4** Tony Pleavin / FailteIreland ; **40 bg1** City of Chicago ; **40 b2** Visitbritain ; **40 b3** Discover San Francisco ; **40 bd4** Visitbritain ; **41** Jktu_21 / SHUTTERSTOCK ; **43 g d** Visit England ; **43 mg md** Visitbritain ; **48 g md d** Visitbritain ; **48 mg** Jameson / Image.net ; **52 h d** Lee Narraway / Nunavut Tourism **h g** Curtis Jones / NunavutTourism **b d** Nunavut Tourism **b g** Nunavut Tourism ; **57 hd b** FailteIreland ; **57 g** City of Chicago **; 60** iStock/spillover ; **63 h mg md** New Zealand Tourism.

N° d'éditeur : 10222798 - Mai 2016
Achevé d'imprimer en France par l'imprimerie Clerc